Happiness
A Gift from God

- being happy is your life mission -

Wisdom of Japanese Philosopher

HIROHISA TOKUO

HIROHISA TOKUO

Babel Corporation

Happiness -A Gift from God-

Published by Babel Corporation, 2012.
All rights reserved.
ISBN: 978-0-9836402-1-9

Author   Hirohisa Tokuo
Translator   Rieko Sasaki

Editor (Original Japanese Version)
              Yoichi Suehiro
              Yoko Shimomura

Illustrator   Yuko Yagami
              Korefumi Ogata

Babel Corporation

Pacific Business News Bldg.#208,
1833 Kalakaua Avenue, Honolulu, Hawaii 96815, USA
Phone: (808) 946-3773
Fax: (808) 946-3993
Website: www.babel.edu

Contents

Foreword · · · · · · · · · · · · · · · · ·6

A Box of God in Egypt   · · · · · · ·7
- Discovery of God as Emptiness and Nothingness

Our Souls Embrace the Cosmos and God, · · ·43
and are also Embraced by God

Afterword · · · · · · · · · · · · · · · · ·72

Foreword

You can read this book in 10 minutes.

Yet you might take 30 years to understand.

From the depths of my heart,
I present this book for you to create your eternal happy life.

The first people you encounter in your life:
your mother, your father, and your siblings.

The first encounter with the girls and boys in your neighborhood.

The first encounter with your teachers, friends, relatives,
customers, bosses, co-workers or foreigners.

All of these encounters are not by chance
but have a certain inevitability.

And then, there is that encounter with the person
who changes your life dramatically and makes you happy.

When you wish to be with that person forever,
when your soul says
"I am the happiest in the world because I met you",

then this is the book for you.

A Box of God in Egypt
- Discovery of God as Emptiness and Nothingness

In the tomb of Tutankhamen in Egypt,
there was a 'box of God'.

It had been undisturbed for 3,300 years.
The box was thought to contain God.

It's now exhibited in the Egyptian Museum in Cairo.
It is small – about 10cm high and 5cm on each side.

The man who first discovered the tomb of Tutankhamen was Howard Carter, a British Egyptologist.

He tried to open the box ...

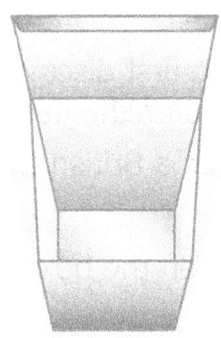

He slowly opened the box.....

It was empty.
... Nothing was inside.

It is a very philosophical answer.

· · · · ·

On January 1, 1996,
My wife and I took a flight
from Greece to Egypt.
We arrived at Cairo airport.

It was a mystical timing.
Jesus was born in B.C. 4.
1996 was the 2000th anniversary of his birth.

My wife and I together
entered the antechamber
where the tomb of Tutankhamen was.

The tomb is located in a valley near Luxor.
There it hardly ever rains.
There is absolutely no plant life.
It is just dry.
It is called the Valley of the Kings.

I am sure that you will also have a chance
to go there in the future.

The tomb was designed to thwart tomb robbers.
It goes very deep into the ground.

However, because of the extreme dryness,
the colors on walls are still vivid and beautiful.
It is very religious.
There are many other tombs in the valley.
Just awesome.

You know,

'Emptiness' is God.
God is 'emptiness'.
'Nothingness' itself is God.

I love this philosophy.
Because the Japanese God is
also 'emptiness and nothingness'.

There is no need to pray to idols.
Shape is never necessary.

'Emptiness' in the small box,
'Emptiness' in the big cosmos,
they are all the same.

There, energy exists.
Also, invisible laws exist.
Atoms always exist
as a structure of electrons, protons, and neutrons.
Energy eternally exists
as a form of particles and waves.

This big 'emptiness' is God.
In other words, 'nothingness' is God.
The vastness of the cosmos is God.
Love, the great wave is God itself.

Nothingness, emptiness, space, waves, particles, energy, laws, love, life.

They are all **God.**

God creates the cosmos and human beings from nothing.
God is 'nothingness' embracing the whole cosmos.
There is no fixture in time or space in nothingness.

God is the existence that can see each single electron in our heart
from the whole cosmos.

Nothingness,
the cosmos existing in the vast space and
that can see right into all human beings' minds;
that is God.

Wherever your truthful heart is, there is your happiness.

Each of our lives is also God.

Jesus, the Buddha, Muhammad are
all masters telling you how this system works.

God is truly invisible.
You cannot tell how big it is.

It is 'nothingness' embracing the whole cosmos.

That is why
you need to listen carefully,
you need to listen with your inner heart,
listen intently to the will of God.

If God is visible,
it is 'nothingness',
it is a tiny little light, and
it is a bright light greater than the galaxy.

Our souls are not our own possession.
They are the souls from the will of heaven.

In the beginning, the Word already existed.

Cherish such words.
Because they are surely a part of God's will.

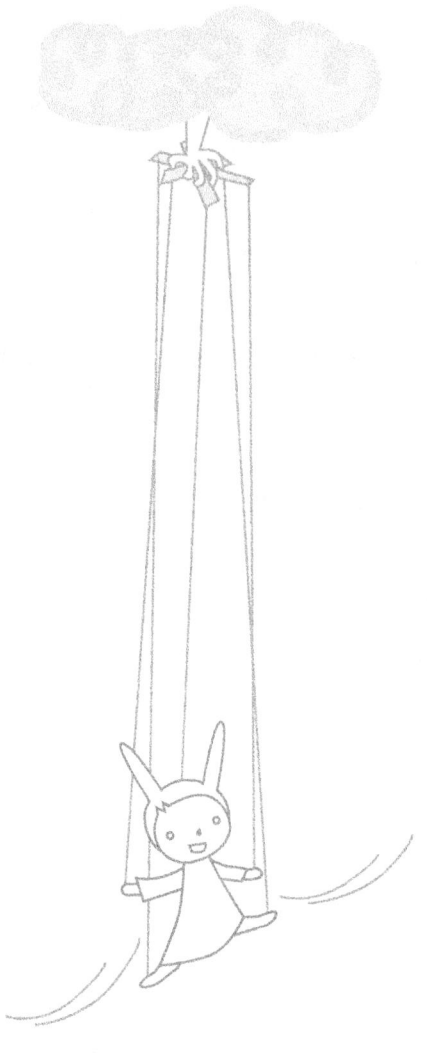

Our intuitions also
come from the 'Great Emptiness'.
They are from God.

Eternal nothingness always
exists in every part of our body,
inside of our body and outside of our body.

It is seeing straight through all of our hearts.

Our Souls Embrace the Cosmos and God, and are also Embraced by God

Human beings physically exist
in the cosmos and the world of the soul.
Our souls exist not only within our bodies.
Our souls are not an organ.

The Form of Life

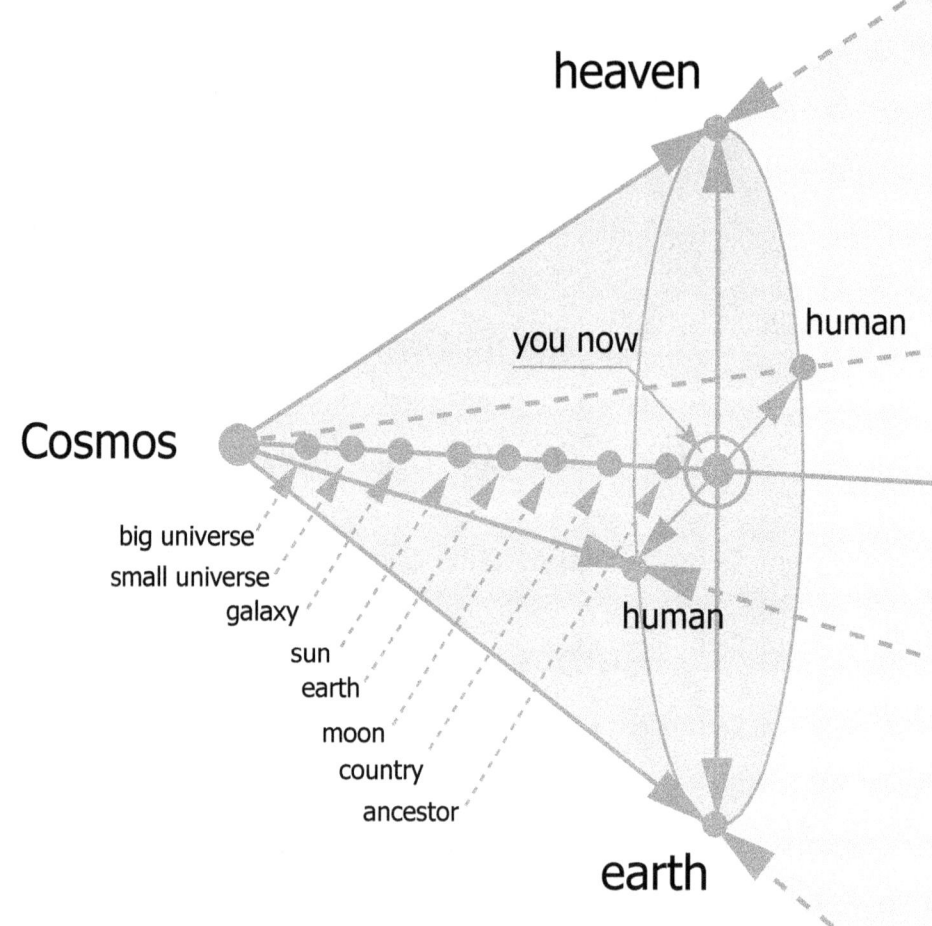

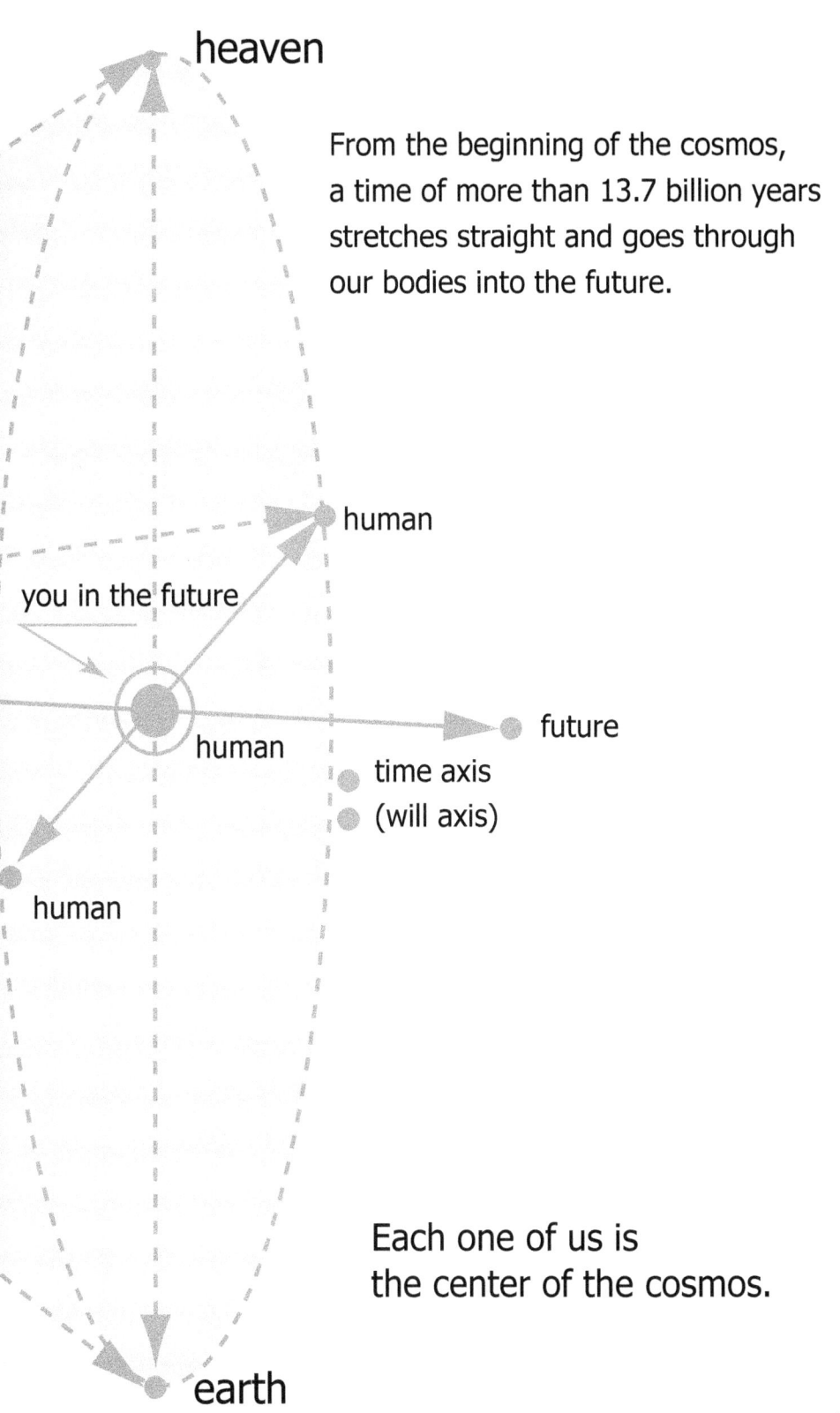

Even in times

when you are busy

do not forget about the longer scale of time

Think about long periods of time
for each event or knowledge.
You will see your eternal soul loving others.

Your destiny is determined by

your words, will,

and actions

There are beautiful positive words and glum negative words.
Even in tough times, first accept your situation,
find out the true value from there,
use positive words, see yourself in the future
and act positively.
Have beautiful images and beautiful words
to enrich your precious life.

We are all honest

to our inner souls

Be true to your inner soul.
Make a sincere effort
on the long journey of your life.
Then success will always come to you.
You can grow, be healthy, and have a stable mind.

Revitalize your mind

every single day

to live young and fresh

Your inner voice is always telling you and directing you
to the path of happiness.
That path does not exist for you
to sacrifice yourself, to live for someone's expectations,
not even to make yourself fit another person's values.
Nobody knows but you
where the true path of your happiness is.

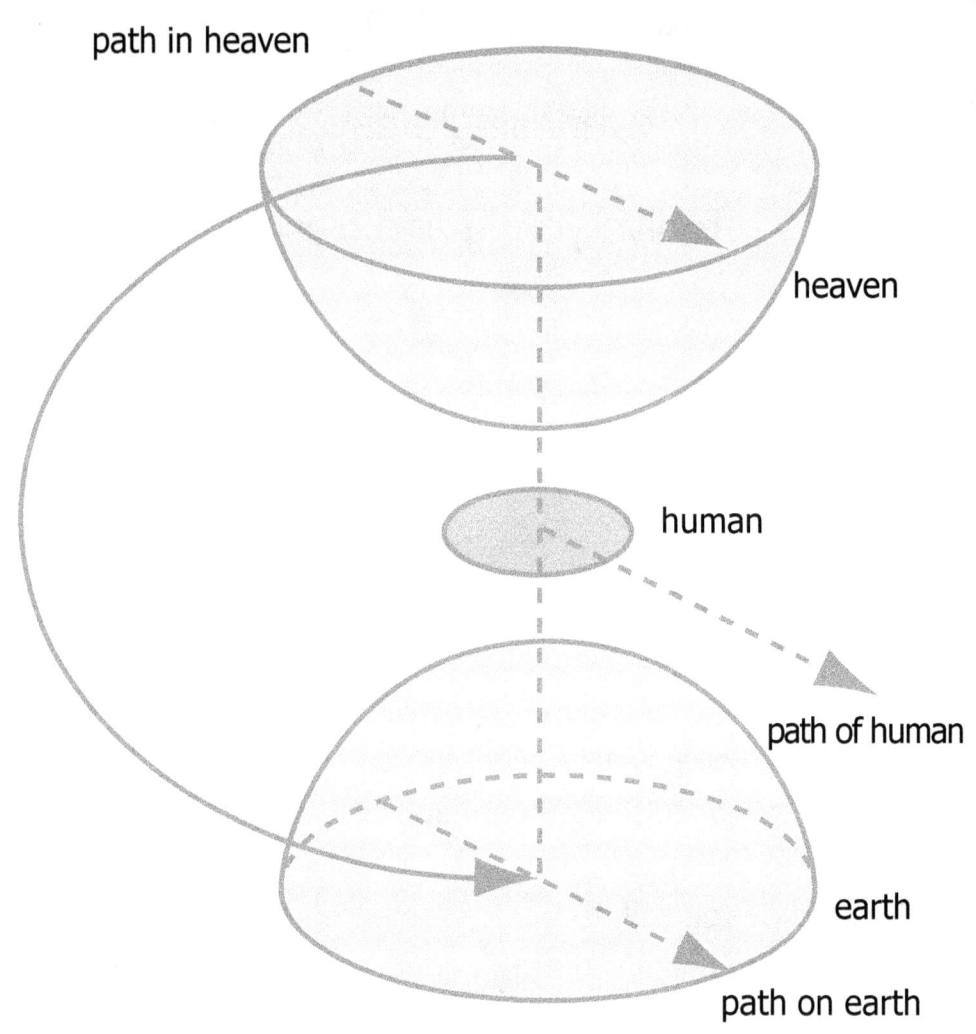

Each one of us is

the center of the cosmos

Heaven is always

smiling at you

A seed grows into a plant

A flower blooms

It turns into another seed

and falls to the ground

That seed grows into a new plant

A flower blooms

And it turns into another seed

Just as snow falls silently,

life is always sacred

Heaven gives

each of us

our precious lives

and wishes them

to be beautiful

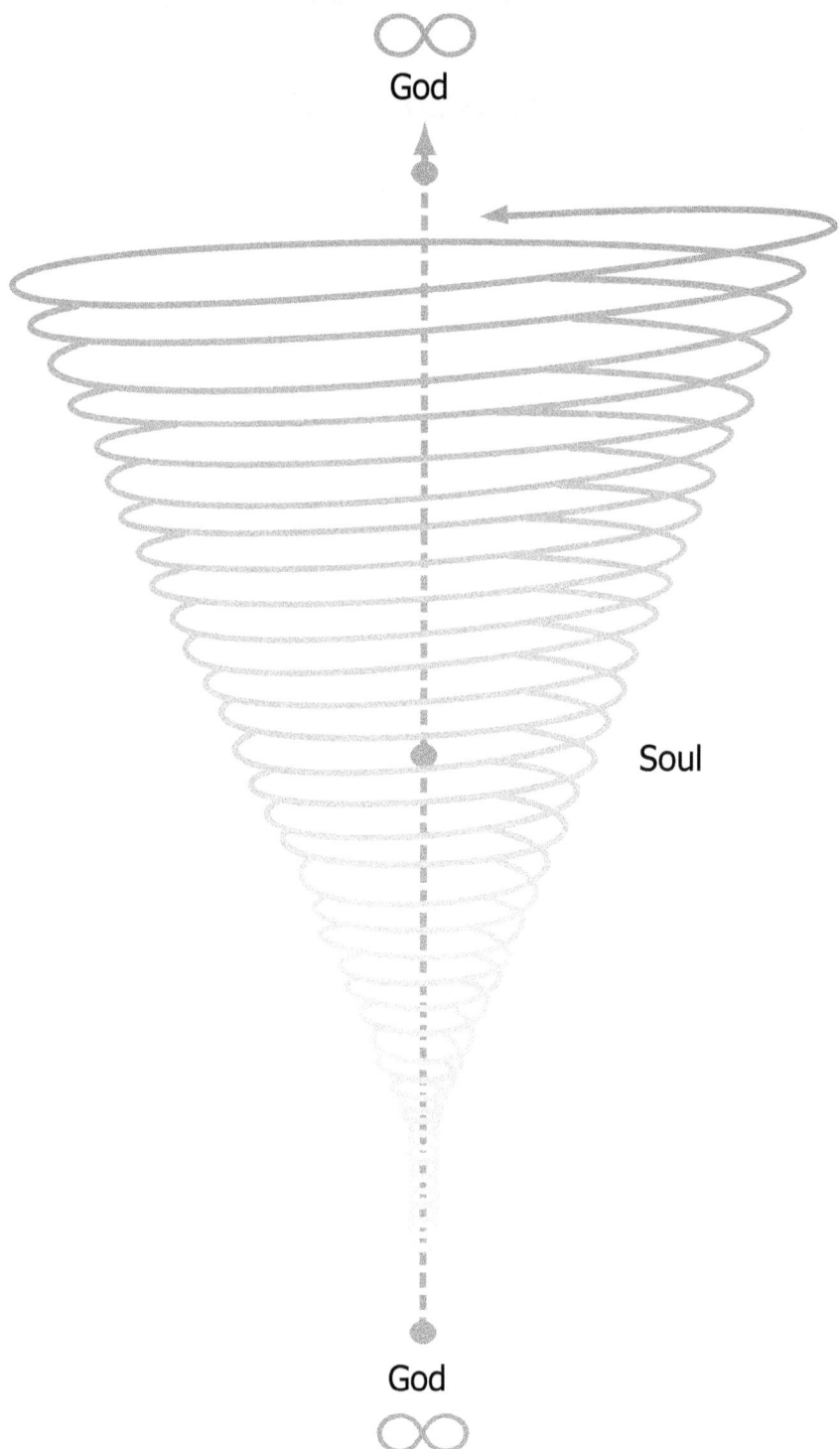

God, heaven sprit, future oriented mind

      big universe
    small universe
       galaxy
   united nations
       world
    international
       nation   Earth, galaxy,
      society
    community   small universe,
     company
      family   big universe,
     individual

                  human beings are
     conscious
integrated conscious   all created
    subconscious
       love   within an enormous sphere.
     [dream]
 (universal mind)
      human   Even the little movement of
     parents
     ancestor   just one finger,
      plants
     animals   all things are
      nature
      moon   working together.
      earth
       sun
      galaxy
  small universe
   big univrese
    particles

       God

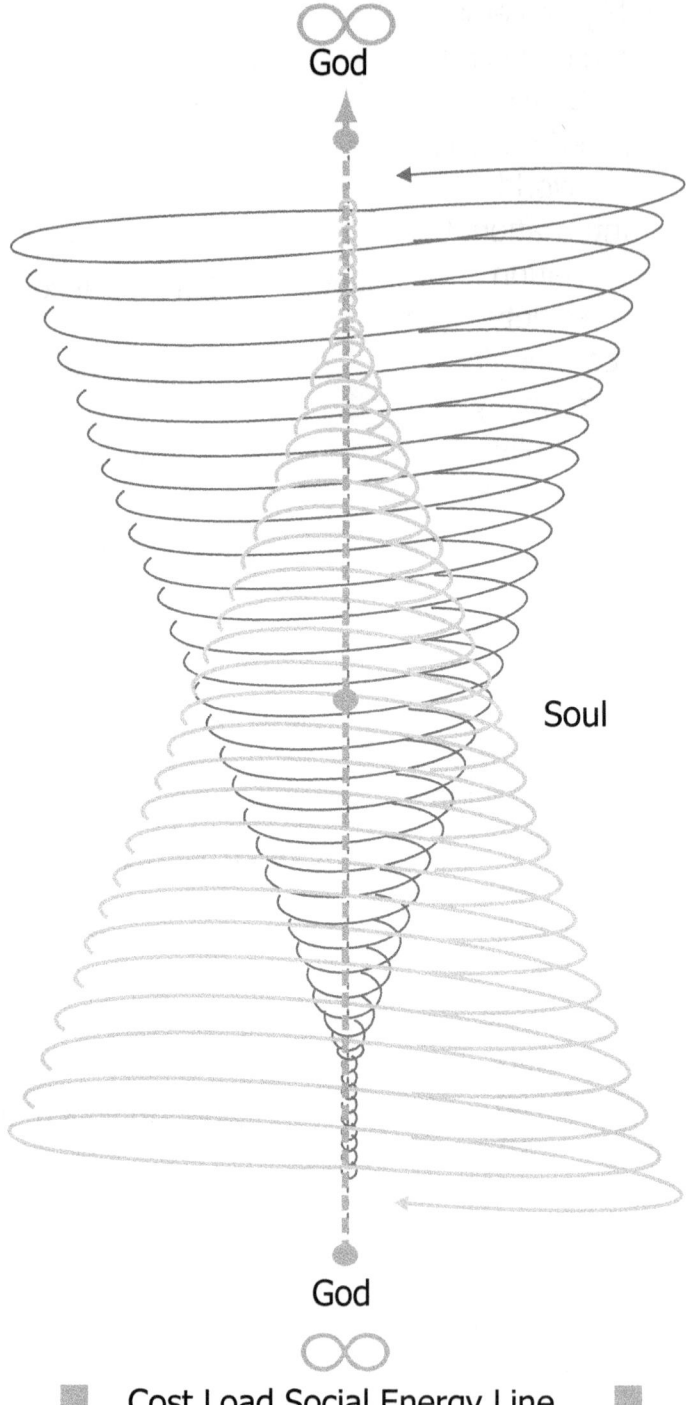

God, heaven sprit, future oriented mind

big universe
small universe
galaxy
united nations
world
international
nation
society
community
company
family
individual

conscious
integrated conscious
subconscious
love
[dream]
(universal mind)
human
parents
ancestor
plants
animals
nature
earth
moon
sun
galaxy
small universe
big univrese
particles

God

The Law of Spiral Evolution by Basic Sentence Patterns

(The word evolution to integrate nature, society and life science)

Evolution of the grammer for world civilization

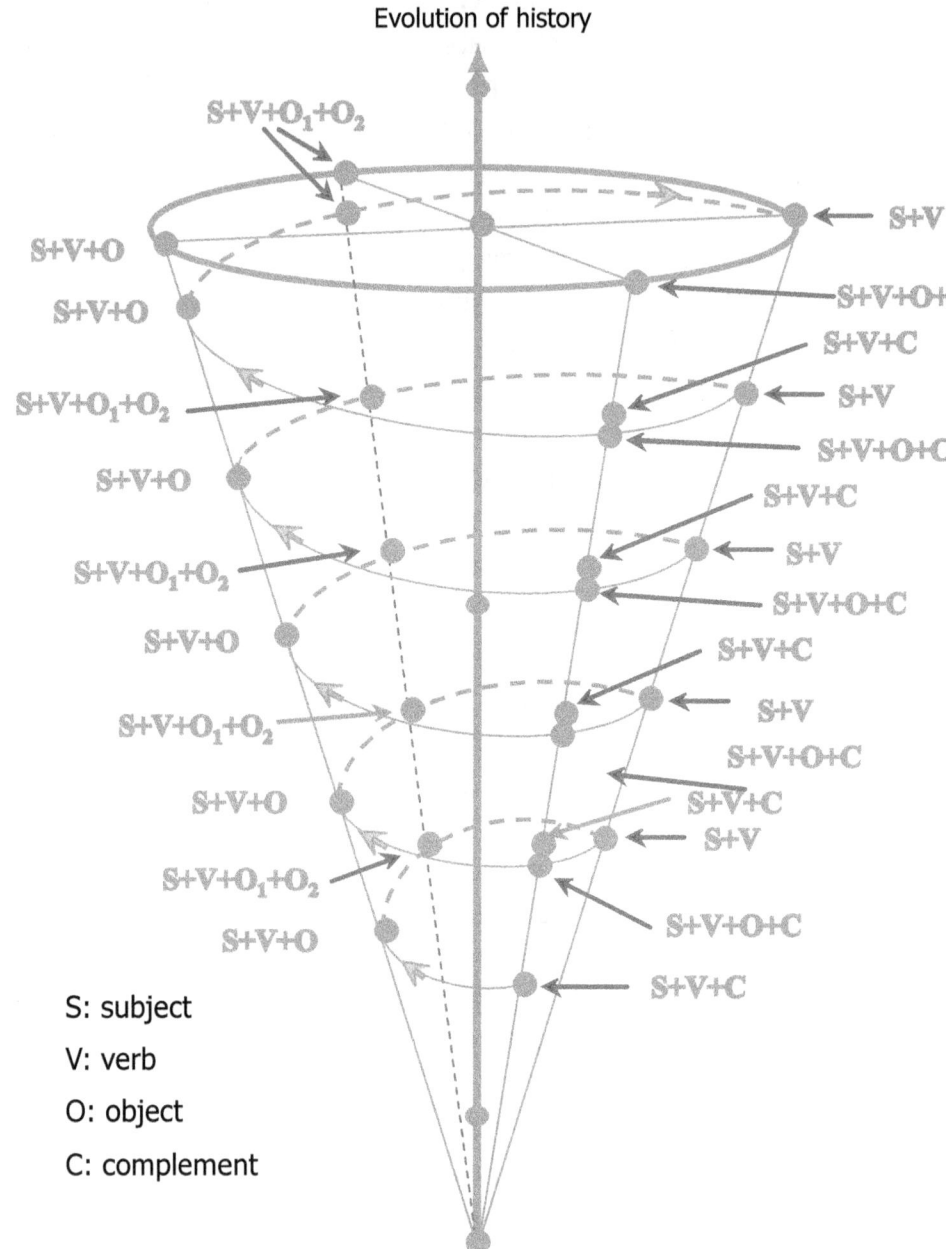

S: subject
V: verb
O: object
C: complement

"In the beginning, the word already existed."

There are grammars for atoms, cells,

health, married life, business management,

politics, and civilization;

they are all simple and they all work

based on the form of

the Spiral Five Basic Sentence Patterns.

Do not feel down

Do not feel failure

Do not feel fear

Live honestly, sincerely and beautifully.
You will succeed and enrich your life.
It doesn't matter how much knowledge you have.
All that matters is how beautiful your mind is.

Even in times of difficulty

do not think that

things are difficult

Thinking widely brings you hints or solutions.
Open your mind wide.
Make many rooms in your heart for 'emptiness'.
Create bright images of your future
and put them in each room.
When you do this, you will win.

The world is filled with treasure

Your happiness does not exist outside of you.
It is inside you.
The things that exist in you flow to the outside world.
If you are filled with beautiful things,
if you are filled with love,
the world where you live will be filled with treasure.

Thinking means

thinking beautifully

Think colorfully, dimensionally

and dynamically

Beautiful people think beautifully.
That is why
they are beautiful and strong
and can act quickly.

The Form of the Cosmos

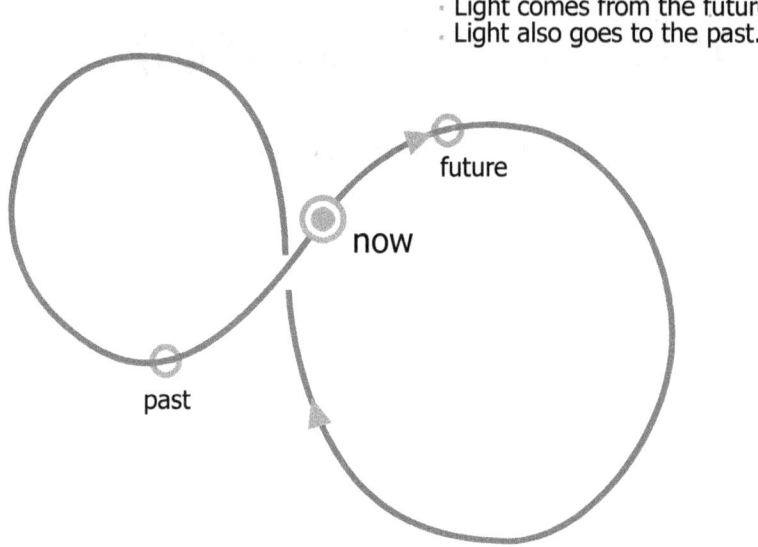

God created the cosmos.

The cosmos created human beings.

Human beings create dreams.

The Form of the Evolution of the Cosmos

Every thing is nothing. Nothing is everything.

(The Heart Sutra)

Transmigration of the expansion and evolution
of the cosmos from big-bang to black box

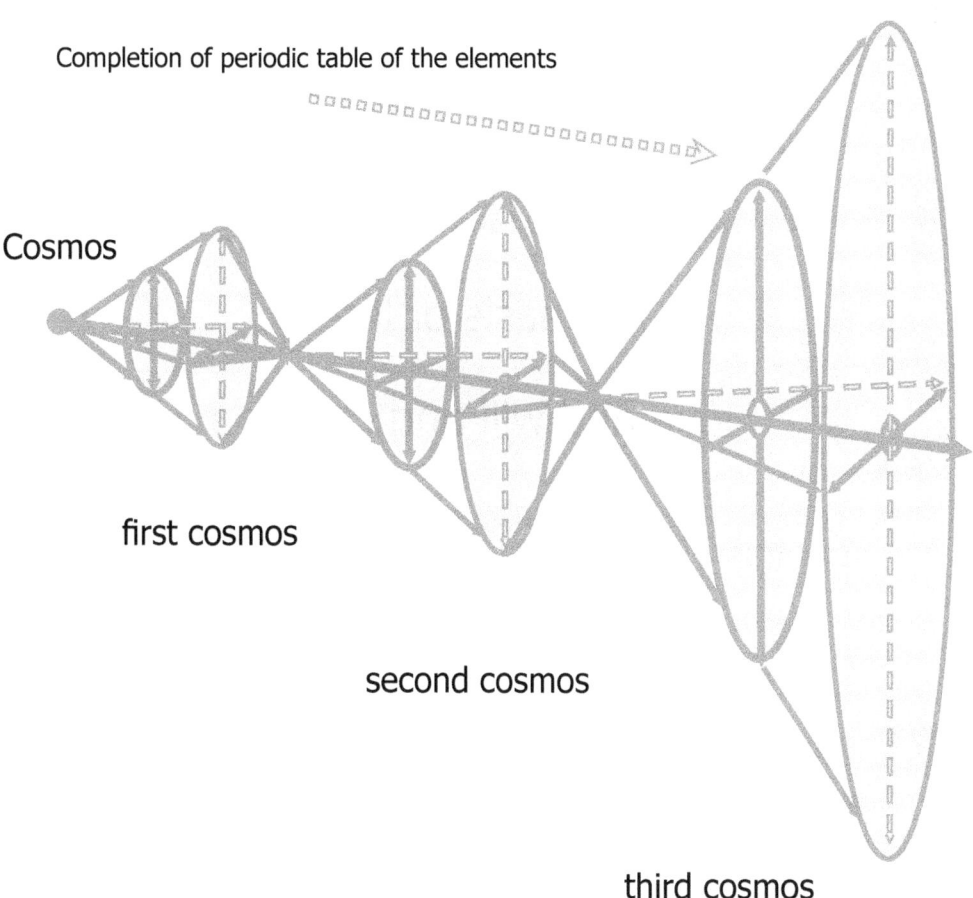

The basis of life is

love and will and creation

Authentic people

are always speaking calmly

using gentle words

The feeling of beautiful happiness

makes your smile beautiful

The beauty of your smile comes from
the strength of your intuition.
You were born to enjoy
the feeling of beautiful happiness.

Begins with love

Ends with love

Love is life

Life is love

Be gentle to others.
It brings you great relationships with them.
Cherish your given life.
Cherish your words.
Open your mind wide.
Be successful with everyone.

Afterword

On the evening of August 9th in 1974, when I was 25 years old, I discovered and illustrated the first world common grammar, Three Dimensional Grammar, which applies to all languages. If you think about the subconscious and creativity using words of three dimensions and draw an entire picture of your life, mind, and words, the circuit of your mind can be the form of intelligence. By thinking about your words as three dimensions and seeing them from the points of function, shape, and cost, you can improve your creativity.

There are many problems we now face around the world. We can find what to do with them if we view the problems from the point of view of the cosmos. Using the same vision, I described and visualized the grammar of problem solving to have a happy married life.

I talked about God in this book. Some may call it 'The Great Existence'. Others may call it 'The Creator'. Whatever you call it, the core essence would not change. If people ask me what God is, I would say it is Nothingness, Beingness, Spirit, Energy of Love, Words, Laws, Cosmos, and Humans; all of the eight elements are God.

With regard to one of the elements, 'Words', we live our lives by learning and using words. People meet people, love each other, get married, have children, and make a family. This is the ideal of happiness. However, sometimes it is difficult to do so.

I studied methods of life problem solving using the grammar of words. I studied the words scientifically to create a happy life. This book was born as the conclusion of my study.

There is a certain cycle of basic sentence forms to solve the problems of life. The point is to change adjectives to transitive verbs and intransitive verbs. It is also important to think and act independently rather than to be controlled by others.

These words create coordinates in our minds. You can create your life beautifully by using positive and future oriented words. There is a certain grammar in the law of marriage. We can create a happy married life by using beautiful words.

It took 37 years to make this book. For publishing the original Japanese version, I would like to express my deepest gratitude to Noriko Kubooka, the president of JDC Publishing, Japan, and her staff. For publishing this English translated version, I am truly grateful to people of Babel K.K., the president Miyoko Yuasa, the executive director Tomoki Hotta, Junko Rodriguez, Sota Torigoe and the translator Rieko Sasaki. Many thanks also go to my wife, Tomoko. I can't thank her enough for her support, understanding, and love through my entire life.

At the dawn of the new millennium of internationalization, I would like to dedicate this work to you. I wish all you readers happiness forever from the bottom of my heart.

Treasure yourself,

Hirohisa Tokuo

Translator's remark

How do you face and handle each difficulty that happens in your life? People say the key to the door to happiness is always hidden in a difficult situation. But when we encounter something tough, where can we look for our door of happiness? How can we open it?

Words that we use can hurt but can also heal people's hearts. Words we use toward others will always return to ourselves. That is why we want to fill our daily lives with beautiful words. Sometimes it is very difficult to do. But actually, in such tough times, the true value of our souls may be tested.

Through this translation work, I was very much encouraged by the author Hirohisa Tokuo. His warm words, gentle smiles, and generous heart which could enfold everything made me realize how much power is hidden in words we use every single day. I am thankful beyond measure for his support and help.

I wish also to express my gratitude to Babel group's wonderful people; the president Miyoko Yuasa, the executive director Tomoki Hotta, the project manager Junko Rodriguez, and the technical expert Sota Torigoe. A big thank you goes to my husband and daughter, too. This book would never been possible without the knowledge, advice, and support from all of them.

And a very special thank you goes out to all of you readers. I understand everybody has their own situation. I hope this book will be the key to open your door of happiness. Please take your time and enjoy this book from your point of view.

With my deepest love and respect,

Rieko Sasaki

Author's Profile

Hirohisa Tokuo was born in 1948. He is a descendant of the chief priest of the Nitta Shrine. The shrine is dedicated to Niniginomikoto, a grandson of Amaterasu (the powerful sun goddess of Japan). It is also famous for when the Heisei emperor and empress visited.

He has dedicated his efforts to studying about how people can be happy from the point of word usage called 'Happy Grammar'. His relative, Toshihiko Tokuo, is also a grammarian who wrote French and Italian grammar books published by Daigaku Shorin.

Tokuo graduated from the School of Agriculture at Kyushu University and received a master's degree in agricultural economics. He also completed courses at the school of Scientific Journalist owned by Katsuhiko Hayashi, a scientific expert and editorial supervisor of NHK TV program "Jintai no Uchu" (The Universe of Human Body).

Tokuo has worked at Asahi Mutual Life Insurance Co., and Tanabe Management Consulting Co., Ltd. He was also the executive director at Shigeki Uniform Co., as well as the manager of management and planning department, the corporate secretary, and the head of audit office of Japan Excel-Management Consulting Co., Ltd. He is currently the president of Tokuo Life Insurance Office.

In addition to his professional career, he was a researcher at the Media Literacy Research Center of Kokusai Gakuin Saitama Junior College.

His publication "The Establish of International Nursing Care Nightingale University" was awarded in 1990 as the excellent paper by Okegawa City at the city's 20th anniversary.

Personal motto: Boys, be ambitious!

Hobbies: Reading, aerobics, and travel. (At the age of 21, he travelled around Japan in 30 days. He has visited 16 countries including Greece and Egypt.)

Publications:
"Sanjigenjiku keiei" (Three Dimensional Management),
Noma Research Institute Inc., May 1990.

Contact:
hirotoku@graces.dricas.com
http://www.sekaibunpo.com/
http://www.tokuo.com/
http://www.facebook.com/

hirotoku@graces.is.dream.jp
http://www.koufuku-bunpo.com/
http://www.sbibusiness.com/pub/090941180